Date Due

FEB 3 1997		
MAR 1 1 1997		
FEB 2 7 1998		
MAR 0 6 2002		
FEB 2 4 2010		
JUL 1 9 2010		

BOOKER T.
WASHINGTON

Educator and Leader

Jack L. Roberts

GATEWAY CIVIL RIGHTS
THE MILLBROOK PRESS
BROOKFIELD, CONNECTICUT

A classroom at the Tuskegee Institute, founded by Booker T. Washington.

Photographs courtesy of UPI/Bettmann: cover background, pp. 7, 8, 17, 18, 25; Library of Congress: cover inset, p. 29; The Schomburg Center: pp. 1, 2-3, 23, 27; Carver Museum, Tuskegee University: pp. 4, 30; Hampton University Archives: p. 12; Tuskegee University Archives, photos by Hawkins Studio: pp. 15, 21, 28.

Library of Congress Cataloging-in-Publication Data
Roberts, Jack L.
Booker T. Washington : educator and leader
Jack L. Roberts.
p. cm—(Gateway civil rights)
Includes bibliographical references and index.
Summary: A biography of the noted black educator, spokesman, and writer.
ISBN 1-56294-487-8
I. Washington, Booker T., 1856-1915—Juvenile literature.
2. Afro-Americans—Biography—Juvenile literature.
3. Educators—United States—Biography—Juvenile literature. [1. Washington, Booker T., 1856-1915. 2. Teachers. 3. Afro-Americans—Biography.] I. Title.
II. Series.
E185.97.W4R63   1995
370´.92—dc20   [B]   94-21484   CIP   AC

Published by The Millbrook Press, Inc.
2 Old New Milford Road, Brookfield, Connecticut 06804

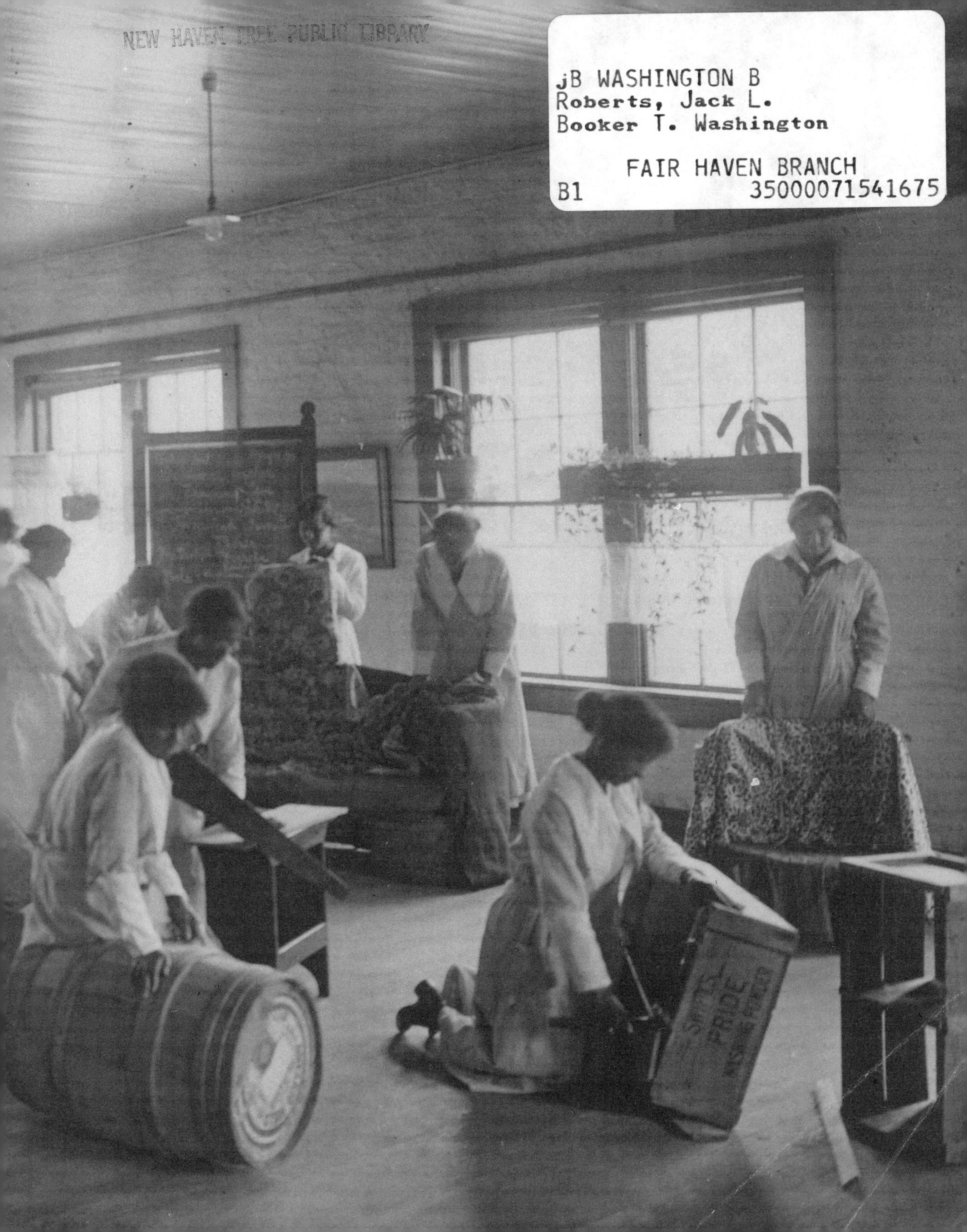
PRIDE

Portrait of Booker T. Washington, by William E. Scott.

The year was 1897. Forty-one-year-old Booker T. Washington sat on the stage of the Academy of Music in Richmond, Virginia. He had been invited there by the people of Richmond to give a speech. It was the first time that a black person was allowed to speak in this great hall.

Washington was the leading spokesman of African Americans throughout the United States. He was a famous teacher and the founder of an important school for black students called the Tuskegee Institute in Tuskegee, Alabama. He was also a former slave. From the time he was born until he was nine years old, he was owned by a white man.

As Washington waited to begin his speech, he thought about the last time he had been in Richmond. He had been a sixteen-year-old boy, passing through Richmond on his way to Hampton, Virginia, where he hoped to go to college.

Back then, many people from his hometown had thought he was foolish. How could a former slave expect to go to college? But Booker had been determined to get an education ever since he was a very young boy.

When young Booker had reached Richmond, he was tired and he was broke. He wandered the streets for hours, looking for a place to spend the night. Finally, around midnight, he came upon a sidewalk made of wooden planks that was raised about two feet above the street. He crawled under the sidewalk and tried to go to sleep. He was kept awake, though, by the sound of people walking on the sidewalk above his head.

Now, as he sat on the stage of this beautiful building in Richmond, Washington thought about that lonely night twenty-five years before.

Suddenly, he heard himself being introduced. He walked to the center of the stage to deliver his speech. It was a speech about hope. He told the audience that there was never a time in his life when he had felt more hopeful for black Americans than he did at that moment.

Washington also thanked the people of Richmond—both black and white. "From the bottom of my heart," he said, "I thank both races for this welcome back to the state that gave me birth."

The Early Years

On April 5, 1856, a baby boy was born into slavery on the James Burroughs plantation in Franklin County, Virginia. His mother, Jane Ferguson, named her young son Booker.

Booker's owners were not as cruel as many slave owners. Yet from the time he was a young boy, Booker had to work very hard. Every day, he cleaned the farmyards and carried water to the men in the fields. In the summer, he would go to

Booker's family home on the Burroughs's plantation in Franklin County, Virginia.

the "big house," where the owner lived, to fan the flies away from the dinner table.

James Burroughs had two daughters who were about the same age as Booker. Often Booker would carry their books to the local one-room schoolhouse. Then he would stand outside looking in. As he watched the young boys and girls study their lessons, he secretly wished that he, too, could go to school.

"I had the feeling," Booker later said, "that to get into a schoolhouse and study in this way would be about the same as getting into paradise."

By the time Booker was five years old, Virginia and ten other Southern states had seceded, or withdrawn, from the Union. They formed the Confederate States of America. In 1861 the Northern states entered into the Civil War with the Confederacy. Northerners wanted to unite the states once again and to end slavery.

This is one of the several black regiments that fought for the North during the Civil War.

For the next four years, the Civil War raged throughout the South. Finally, one morning in 1865, the master of the plantation called the slaves to the "big house." There, a man read an important document called the Emancipation Proclamation. It had been signed by Abraham Lincoln, president of the United States. "I do order and declare that all persons held as slaves shall be free," President Lincoln said.

Booker's mother leaned down and kissed her children, as tears of joy ran down her cheeks. She told them that this was the day she had long been praying for, "but fearing she would never live to see."

At long last, Booker and his family were free.

Life as a Young Boy

During the Civil War, Booker's stepfather, Washington Ferguson, had run away from his owners. Wash, as he was called, had settled in Malden, West Virginia. Now that the slaves were free, Wash had his family join him. He then forced Booker and his older brother to go to work in the salt mines. Booker was not yet ten years old.

A few months later, a private school for black children was opened in the town of Malden. Booker begged his stepfather to let him attend. Finally, his stepfather agreed, but only as long as the young boy continued to work part-time in the mines.

On his first day of school, Booker discovered that all of the other children had two names, sometimes even three. Booker had never had a last name. So when the teacher called the roll, he made one up. He decided to call himself Booker Washington. Later, he learned that his mother had given him the name Booker Taliaferro (pronounced "Tolliver") when he was born, so he became Booker T. Washington.

When Booker was a little older, his stepfather made him go to work in the coal mines. Booker hated working there and later said it was one of the most miserable periods of his life.

One day, when he was deep in the mines, Booker heard two men talking about a special school called the Hampton Normal and Agricultural Institute in Hampton, Virginia. It was a three-year college that trained young black students for jobs in farming or education or industry. Poor students could work at the school to pay for all or part of their education.

From that moment on, Booker dreamed about going there. "Although I had no idea where it was, or how many miles away, or how I was going to reach it," Booker later recalled, "I was on fire constantly with one ambition, and that was to go to Hampton."

Finally, in the fall of 1872, Booker decided it was time to fulfill his dream and go to the Hampton Institute. He had almost no money; he wasn't even sure how to get there. Nevertheless, he set out on a journey that would change his life forever.

The Hampton Institute

When Booker arrived at the Hampton Institute that October, he had exactly fifty cents in his pocket. Yet, he later said about that special day, "I felt I had reached the promised land."

Booker wanted to begin class immediately. But first the assistant principal wanted to find out if he was a good worker. If so, he could work in exchange for his room and board. To test him, she handed him a broom and told him to sweep one of the classrooms.

Booker swept the room three times. He also dusted every corner of the room and every piece of furniture. He was determined to make it cleaner than it had ever been. When he was done, the assistant principal came into the room to inspect it. She checked everything carefully. At last, she looked at Booker and said, "I guess you will do to enter this institution." Booker was thrilled.

Booker at the Hampton Institute, where he learned many of the important lessons of his life.

During his three years at the Institute, Booker worked as a janitor to help pay for his room and board. "This work was hard and taxing," Washington later said. "I had to work late into the night, while at the same time I had to rise by four o'clock in the morning, in order to build the fires and have a little time in which to prepare my lessons."

Booker learned something at the school that did not come out of a textbook. He learned to love work. And years later, he often talked about the dignity of labor. "I have had no patience with any school which did not teach its students the dignity of labor," he once said.

At the end of his second year, Washington returned to Malden to spend the summer with his family. During that visit his mother died.

He returned to school in the fall determined to do the very best he could in spite of his sorrow. When he graduated in June 1875, he was on the honor roll.

Early Career

Soon after he graduated, Washington took a job as a teacher at the black school in Malden. He worked many long hours each day. Yet Washington often said that this was one of the happiest periods of his life. "I had the opportunity to help the people of my home town to a higher life."

In the summer of 1879, Washington received a letter from the head of the Hampton Institute, General Samuel C. Armstrong. General Armstrong wanted Washington to take part in a bold educational experiment.

In those days, many people did not believe that Native Americans had the intelligence or ability to learn. Armstrong felt differently. So he invited one hundred young Indians to the school.

Armstrong wanted Washington to serve as a house father, or counselor, to these students and also to teach them English. Washington, who felt honored to be offered the job, accepted. He soon discovered that once the Indians started to learn English, they were able to learn other subjects as quickly as other students. Armstrong's experiment was a success.

In his second year as a teacher at the Hampton Institute, Washington was asked to head another new program. This was a night school for students whose jobs kept them from going to school during the day. Within no time at all, Washington had twenty-five students.

In May 1881, General Armstrong called Washington into his office. Alabama had recently passed a bill to establish a school for black students in the small town of Tuskegee, 130 miles (40 kilometers) south of Atlanta. They needed someone to run the school. "Would you be interested in the position?" Armstrong asked Washington.

Washington thought long and hard about the offer. Finally, he decided to accept the position. It was a decision he would never regret.

The Beginning of the Tuskegee Institute

When Washington arrived in Tuskegee in June of 1881, he was ready and eager to begin teaching. There was just one problem. There was no school building in Tuskegee where he could hold classes.

That didn't stop Washington. He found an old building, or shanty, that belonged to the black church in town. This run-down building became the Tuskegee Institute, and the school opened its doors to thirty students on July 4.

At Tuskegee, courses such as this one in shoemaking taught students practical skills.

From the beginning, the Tuskegee Institute taught academic subjects, such as English and math. It also taught vocational subjects, such as how to grow cotton or build a house. As Washington explained, the teachers wanted to make sure that their students "would know how to make a living after they had left us."

Soon after the school opened, Washington borrowed $200 as a down payment to buy a 100-acre plantation. The main house had been badly burned during the Civil War, but Washington knew the property would make a perfect campus. By the end of the first year, the school had grown to include more than one hundred students.

That summer, Washington returned to Malden. There, on August 2, 1882, he married his childhood sweetheart, Fanny N. Smith. The following summer, on June 6, 1883, Fanny gave birth to a daughter. They named their child Portia Marshall Washington.

Less than a year later, on May 4, 1884, Fanny died, perhaps because of injuries caused by a fall from a farm wagon. Washington was greatly saddened by her death. But he had a young daughter to raise and an important school to maintain. So he continued with his work.

In May 1885, Tuskegee Institute held its first graduation exercises. Washington was extremely proud. And he had every right to be. As one newspaper reported, "Tuskegee is the most successful effort of the Negro at self-education in this country."

Washington, during a speech before the student body at Tuskegee.

Maggie and Booker T. Washington sit outside their Tuskegee home with their sons, Ernest Davidson (left) and Booker T., Jr.

On August 11, 1885, Washington married Olivia A. Davidson. Davidson had become the third teacher at Tuskegee in the fall of 1881. Later, she worked closely with Washington in his fund-raising activities for the school.

On May 29, 1887, Olivia gave birth to their first son, Booker T. Washington, Jr. Two years later, on February 6, 1889, she gave birth to a second son, Ernest Davidson Washington. It was a difficult birth, made worse by the fact that Olivia had been in poor health to begin with. Three months later she died from complications. The entire school mourned her death.

In 1893, Washington married Margaret "Maggie" James Murray. She was twenty-four years old. She had come to teach at Tuskegee several years earlier and later became "Lady Principal."

These were difficult years for the Tuskegee Institute. The school was almost always broke. Washington traveled constantly throughout the country, trying to raise money to keep the school open and to help it grow.

During these years, Washington became a popular guest speaker in some parts of the North and the South. Soon, however, he was to deliver a speech that would make him famous throughout the country.

The Atlanta Speech

In the spring of 1895, Southerners were planning to hold a world's fair called the Atlanta Cotton States and International Exposition to exhibit new products and inventions. Washington was invited to give a speech on opening day, September 18. This was an important invitation. It was the first time a black man was asked to speak from the same stage with white men and women in the South.

Many people were angry about this. They didn't think a black man should be allowed to speak on the same stage as whites. Washington knew he would be speaking for black people everywhere, so he wanted to make a good impression. As he put it, he wanted to say something that would help to "cement the friendship of the races."

During his speech, Washington pledged the support of all black people in helping to work out the differences between the races. He then said something that helped make him the leading spokesman for black people everywhere.

Holding his hand above his head with his fingers spread apart, Washington said: "In all things that are purely social we can be as separate as the fingers." He then clenched his fist and added, "Yet one as the hand in all things essential to mutual progress."

These words, which became known as the Atlanta Compromise, explained in brief Washington's feelings about the relationship between the two races. Many people—both black and white—agreed with him. They believed that the two races could live separately but have equal opportunities.

At the end of Washington's speech, the crowd rose to its feet, applauding and cheering wildly. The next day, newspapers all across the country carried stories about this important speech. One editor said it was one of the most notable speeches ever given to a southern audience.

A few months earlier, Frederick Douglass, the most popular black leader in the country, had died. People wondered who would take his place as a spokesman for African Americans. Now, with this one speech, they had their answer. The new political and social leader of African Americans in both the North and the South was Booker T. Washington.

A Leader for All

For the next few years, Washington was at the height of his popularity. He earned the respect of both blacks and whites. He became an adviser to President William McKinley on matters of race relations and later to Theodore Roosevelt and William Howard Taft.

Washington began speaking to raise money for his school. His reputation spread, and large crowds gathered to hear him speak on racial issues.

In June 1896, Washington also received one of the greatest honors of his life. Harvard University, the oldest university in the United States, gave him an honorary master's degree. It was the first time that a New England university had honored a black man in this way.

When Washington first learned that he was going to receive the degree, he was deeply moved. "Tears came into my eyes," he later said, as he thought about his life as a slave, his struggle for an education, and his difficulties in starting a school for black students.

During these years, Washington traveled nearly six months out of each year, trying to raise money for the school. He also paid very close attention to the needs of the students. In 1896 he invited a young teacher named George Washington Carver to come to Tuskegee to start an agricultural department. Carver, who later became a world-famous scientist, taught at Tuskegee nearly fifty years.

By 1899, Washington was clearly exhausted. He had been working without a vacation for seventeen years. Concerned friends insisted he take a trip to Europe. At first, Washington refused to go. He was afraid people might think that he had become "stuck up," or that he was trying to show off. But finally, he and his wife sailed to Europe for a three-month vacation. During that trip, Washington was invited by Queen Victoria of England to be her guest for tea at Windsor Castle.

GEORGE WASHINGTON CARVER

Like Booker T. Washington, George Washington Carver was born a slave, sometime between 1860 and 1864 in southwest Missouri. Also like Washington, as a young boy Carver was determined to get an education. Often he walked eight miles each way to attend school.

In 1890, Carver heard about Iowa State Agricultural College. Since he had always been interested in plants and flowers, he enrolled there to study botany, the science of plants. He became the first black to graduate from Iowa State.

In 1896, Booker T. Washington invited Carver to start a new department at Tuskegee to teach students about agriculture. For the next forty-seven years, Carver taught students about plants and soil and how to grow bigger and better crops. He also worked hard in his laboratory, inventing new products and new uses for both sweet potatoes and peanuts. He became known as the Wizard of Tuskegee.

Throughout his career, Carver won many awards for his work in science. One special award was given to him by President Franklin D. Roosevelt in 1939.

On January 5, 1943, George Washington Carver died. He had become one of America's most famous scientists.

The End of a Career

During the last fifteen years of his life, Washington continued to work as hard as ever. He not only handled the day-to-day activities involved in running a school, but he also worked every day to promote better relations between blacks and whites.

Washington also worked hard to bring about more economic equality between blacks and whites. In 1900, for example, he helped start and then became president of an organization called the National Negro Business League. This group helped blacks start their own businesses.

The following year, in 1901, Washington published his autobiography, *Up from Slavery*. This moving story was translated into many languages and helped make Washington famous all over the world. It also prompted many wealthy Americans to donate money to Tuskegee. For example, George Eastman, founder of the Eastman-Kodak camera company, donated $10,000 a year to Tuskegee after reading Washington's book.

That same year, Washington accepted an invitation to have dinner at the White House with President Theodore Roosevelt. This was the first time that a black man had ever had dinner with a president and his family at the White House.

Many white Southerners, who had previously supported Washington, were shocked and angry. They said it was socially

Washington, looking determined and successful in
a 1906 photograph by Frances Benjamin Johnston.

unacceptable for a black man and a president to dine on equal
terms in the White House.

By the early 1900s, many blacks and liberal whites began
to disagree with Washington's racial philosophy. They dis-
agreed, for example, with the "separate but equal" approach to
race relations. They also said that Washington did not speak
out strongly enough against white injustices toward blacks. So,
they began to look to other black leaders. One of these leaders
was W.E.B. Du Bois.

Du Bois's racial philosophy was very different from Washington's. Washington accepted segregation; Du Bois opposed it. Washington believed that whites would eventually give blacks equal rights. Du Bois said that blacks should not have to wait to be given their civil rights. Their rights, he said, were guaranteed by the U.S. Constitution.

Gradually, Washington's role as the leading spokesman for all African Americans began to lessen. Yet he continued until the end of his life to fight discrimination and to bring about better relations between blacks and whites. "More and more," he often said during these later years, "we must learn to think not in terms of race or color or language or religion or political boundaries, but in terms of humanity."

By 1910, Washington's health was beginning to fail. During this time, he continued to accept speaking engagements around the country and wrote two other books, *My Larger Education* in 1911 and *The Man Farthest Down* in 1912.

By 1915, Washington was clearly very sick. While on a tour, he checked into a hospital in New York City, where doctors discovered that he was suffering from a serious kidney problem. Washington wanted to return home to Tuskegee, but the doctors told him the trip would kill him. He didn't care. "I was born in the South, I have lived and labored in the South, and I expect to die and be buried in the South."

W.E.B. DU BOIS

William Edward Burghardt Du Bois was born in Great Barrington, Massachusetts, on February 23, 1868. Unlike Washington, Du Bois grew up knowing very little about racism. In 1890 he graduated from Harvard University. For the next few years, he taught at Wilberforce College in Ohio, while he completed his doctorate at Harvard.

As a young man, Du Bois supported Washington. But in 1903 he published *The Souls of Black Folk,* a series of essays that criticized Washington and his views. He felt Washington was wrong to emphasize industrial education for black students. He also did not believe Washington spoke out strongly enough against segregation.

In 1908 a group of blacks and liberal whites formed a group to promote equal rights called the National Association for the Advancement of Colored People (NAACP). Washington was not involved. The NAACP, with Du Bois as one of its leaders, became very powerful, and Washington lost a great deal of influence.

Du Bois took the place of Washington as the spokesperson for blacks, just as Washington had replaced Frederick Douglass.

Booker T. Washington's funeral at the Tuskegee Institute in 1915.

Washington boarded a train and arrived at Tuskegee on the evening of November 13. He died the next day at 4:45 A.M. on November 14, 1915, at the age of fifty-nine.

Thousands of people throughout America and the world mourned his death. Many paid glowing tribute to this former slave who had raised himself up from poverty to become a leader of his people.

Perhaps the greatest tribute, though, came from industrialist Andrew Carnegie, who had helped to support the Tuskegee Institute. "History will know two Washingtons," Carnegie said, referring to George Washington and Booker T. Washington. "Both are fathers of their people."

IMPORTANT DATES IN THE LIFE OF BOOKER T. WASHINGTON

1856   Booker T. Washington is born a slave on a plantation in Franklin County, Virginia.

1865   The Civil War ends; Washington moves to Malden, West Virginia, with his family.

1872   Washington goes to school at the Hampton Institute in Hampton, Virginia. He graduates in 1875.

1879   General Samuel C. Armstrong invites Washington to teach at the Hampton Institute.

1881   Washington opens the Tuskegee Institute in Tuskegee, Alabama.

1895   Washington delivers his famous speech at the Atlanta Cotton States and International Exposition, calling for a "separate but equal" approach to the races.

1901   Washington publishes his autobiography, *Up from Slavery*.

1915   Washington dies in Tuskegee on November 14.

FIND OUT MORE ABOUT
BOOKER T. WASHINGTON

Booker T. Washington by Jan Gleiter and Kathleen Thompson (Austin, Texas: Raintree Steck-Vaughn, 1987).

Booker T. Washington: Leader and Educator by Patricia McKissack and Fredrick McKissack (Hillside, New Jersey: Enslow Publishers, 1992).

Booker T. Washington: Leader of His People by Alan Schroeder (New York: Chelsea House Publishers, 1991).

The Story of Booker T. Washington by Patricia McKissack and Fredrick McKissack (Chicago, Illinois: Childrens Press, 1991).

A statue on the Tuskegee campus
shows Booker T. Washington
"lifting the veil of ignorance."

INDEX